Novice Obedience CD Training

Class and Practice Journal

Mary Jean Simpson

This journal belongs to _____

Acknowledgements

Many people have contributed to my wonderful journey with my dogs. I would like to acknowledge several who have been an especially important part of my journey.

Patty Page, Shetland Sheepdog breeder, entrusted me with my wonderful first Sheltie and with my delightful last Sheltie. She was a mentor, a teacher, and a friend. She got me involved with a Shetland Sheepdog Club where I met other Sheltie folks, made some good friends, and enjoyed many happy events.

Pat Schaap, Sheltie breeder and trainer, became a mentor, a good friend, a teacher, and the breeder of an incredible Sheltie, Zinger, who had a great sense of humor and dearly loved agility.

The late **Ruth Chase**, excellent trainer, with whom we spent many happy hours of instruction. Under her training, Travis earned his CD. She introduced Zinger to agility, a sport he dearly loved.

Nancy Duke, Papillon breeder, breeder of two of my Papillons. She became a mentor and friend and assisted in showing Nova.

Carlotta Denny, Papillon exhibitor who showed Nova and picked up important points on her.

Leslie Nelson, outstanding trainer and owner of Tails-U-Win!, and her **excellent trainers**. With my dogs at various levels, they took us through puppy classes, obedience, and agility training. My dogs and I spent many, many happy times her school.

Photo of My Dog on the First Day

Dog's name _____

Schedule of Classes

Class 1:

Date_____   Time _____

Location _____

_____

Contact Information _____

Type of class or training _____

Trainer _____

What to bring _____

_____

Class 2:

Date_____   Time _____

Location _____

_____

Contact Information _____

Type of class or training _____

Trainer _____

What to bring _____

_____

Class 3:

Date_____ Time _____

Location _____

_____

Contact Information _____

Type of class or training _____

Trainer _____

What to bring _____

_____

Class 4:

Date_____ Time _____

Location _____

_____

Contact Information _____

Type of class or training _____

Trainer _____

What to bring _____

_____

Class 5:

Date_____ Time _____

Location _____

_____

Contact Information _____

Type of class or training _____

Trainer _____

What to bring _____

_____

Class 6:

Date_____ Time _____

Location _____

_____

Contact Information _____

Type of class or training _____

Trainer _____

What to bring _____

_____

Class 7:

Date_____ Time _____

Location _____

_____

Contact Information _____

Type of class or training _____

Trainer _____

What to bring _____

_____

Class 8:

Date_____ Time _____

Location _____

_____

Contact Information _____

Type of class or training _____

Trainer _____

What to bring _____

_____

Some Things You May Need to Take to Class:

For your convenience, a list of possible items you may need or wish to take to your classes is provided below. This list is not exhaustive. Depending upon the level and type of training, what you take may vary from class to class.

This list may be duplicated for your personal use for individual classes.

1. Water and bowl _____

2. High value treats _____

   _____

3. Lead _____

4. Special toy or toys _____

   _____

5. Crate or doggie seat belt _____

6. Vaccination records _____

7. Special articles or equipment _____

   _____

8. Notebook and pen _____

9. Dog—yes, people have gone without the dog! _____

10. Anything else _____

    _____

    _____

    _____

Instructions for Using This Journal

Going to training classes should always be a happy, exciting adventure for both you and your dog. This journal is intended to help make training as enjoyable and free of stress as possible.

The first page of each week is designed to cover the class itself. There is a place for writing down the goals for that training, what was done or learned during the class, and what you are to work on for the following week. The remaining six days allow you to determine what your goal is for that day's practice, what you actually achieve, and any questions or concerns you may wish to bring up at the next class.

It is important to remember that dogs, like people, learn at different rates. Some skills may be achieved very quickly while others may take what seems like a long time. There will be times when your dog will seem to have forgotten something you thought he or she had mastered. Patience and as much repetition as needed will pay off. Suddenly a light will dawn and your dog will perform perfectly.

Remember to keep training sessions short enough for the age and attention span of your dog. Always use positive reinforcement—rewards for success—not punishment. This will keep the training enjoyable and rewarding for you and for your dog.

Pace the learning so that your buddy experiences success. If your pal starts to become bored, take a break and play a favorite game or do something else he or she really enjoys.

When you come back, start with something your pal has already mastered and reward him or her. Then move on to the new training. Patience and practice will result in a well-trained canine citizen who is a pleasure to live with and a true companion for life. Persistence works. Enjoy the journey.

Introduction to Novice Obedience

Having completed your Basic Obedience training, you are ready to move on to Novice Obedience. This is the first of three main levels of Competition Obedience. There are several other classes, some of which do not earn titles, you can compete in, or try different exercises, or just have fun.

Novice level competition obedience is for the dog just getting started in obedience. The judge determines how well a dog has learned the responses to several commands. They include Heel on Leash (Lead) and Figure Eight to show whether the dog has learned to watch the handler and adjust their pace to stay with the handler. Also, the dog must Heel Free, performing a heeling pattern with the dog off-leash.

In the Stand for Examination, the dog must remain in the standing position as the handler walks a short distance away. The judge lightly touches the dog on the head, the body, and the hindquarters, after which the handler returns to the dog. In the Recall, the dog must return to the handler on command. For the one-minute Long Sit, the dog must remain sitting in the presence of other dogs while the handler stands across the ring. The three-minute Long Down requires the dog to remain in a down position in the presence of other dogs while the handler stands across the ring.

Training takes a lot of work. There will be times when progress seems really slow. Just go back to commands your dog has mastered or move to a different command. Always use positive reinforcement. Keep practice to 15 minutes a session at the most, and always end on a positive note. This will make your dog excited and eager to work when practice time returns.

May you and your dog have a wonderful time working toward a CD (Companion Dog) title. Above all, just have fun!

OK, Let's Get Started

You are going to have questions about the training, the class content, how to best work with your dog, and other things that are important to you. Here is space for you to record these questi9ns and concerns so that they are in mind when you want them.

_____

_____

_____

_____

_____

_____

_____

_____

_____

_____

_____

_____

_____

_____

_____

_____

_____

_____

_____

_____

_____

_____

_____

Class 1 Training: Week 1, Day 1

Goals for First Week

_____

_____

_____

_____

_____

Long-Term Goals

_____

_____

_____

_____

_____

What Was Done or Learned During This Class

_____

_____

_____

_____

_____

_____

_____

_____

_____

_____

_____

_____

_____

Assignment for Next Week's Class

_____
_____
_____
_____
_____
_____
_____

What I Need to Focus on With My Dog

_____
_____
_____
_____
_____
_____
_____
_____
_____
_____
_____
_____
_____
_____
_____
_____
_____
_____

Week 1, Day 2

Goals for the Day

_____

_____

_____

_____

_____

_____

Training (What We Did Today, Steps We Took, Length of Each Training Period, Rewards Given for Successes)

_____

_____

_____

_____

_____

_____

_____

_____

_____

_____

_____

_____

_____

_____

_____

_____

_____

_____

_____
_____
_____
_____
_____
_____

What We Accomplished and What Needs More Work

_____
_____
_____
_____
_____
_____
_____
_____
_____
_____
_____
_____
_____
_____
_____

Questions or Concerns

_____
_____
_____
_____

Week 1, Day 3

Goals for the Day

_____

_____

_____

_____

_____

_____

Training (What We Did Today, Steps We Took, Length of Each Training Period, Rewards Given for Successes)

_____

_____

_____

_____

_____

_____

_____

_____

_____

_____

_____

_____

_____

_____

_____

_____

What We Accomplished and What Needs More Work

Questions or Concerns

Week 1, Day 4

Goals for the Day

_____
_____
_____
_____
_____
_____

Training (What We Did Today, Steps We Took, Length of Each Training Period, Rewards Given for Successes)

_____
_____
_____
_____
_____
_____
_____
_____
_____
_____
_____
_____
_____
_____
_____
_____
_____

_____

_____

_____

_____

_____

_____

What We Accomplished and What Needs More Work

_____

_____

_____

_____

_____

_____

_____

_____

_____

_____

_____

_____

_____

_____

_____

Questions or Concerns

_____

_____

_____

_____

Week 1, Day 5

Goals for the Day

_____

_____

_____

_____

_____

_____

Training (What We Did, Steps We Took, Length of Each Training Period, Rewards Given for Successes)

_____

_____

_____

_____

_____

_____

_____

_____

_____

_____

_____

_____

_____

_____

_____

_____

_____

_____

_____

_____

_____

_____

_____

_____

What We Accomplished and What Needs More Work

_____

_____

_____

_____

_____

_____

_____

_____

_____

_____

_____

_____

_____

_____

Questions or Concerns

_____

_____

_____

_____

Week 1, Day 6

Goals for the Day

_____

_____

_____

_____

_____

Training (What We Did Today, Steps We Took, Length of Each Training Period, Rewards Given for Successes)

_____

_____

_____

_____

_____

_____

_____

_____

_____

_____

_____

_____

_____

_____

_____

_____

_____

_____

_____

_____

_____

_____

_____

_____

What We Accomplished and What Needs More Work

_____

_____

_____

_____

_____

_____

_____

_____

_____

_____

_____

_____

_____

_____

_____

_____

Questions or Concerns

_____

_____

_____

_____

Week 1, Day 7

Goals for the Day

_____
_____
_____
_____
_____
_____

Training (What We Did Today, Steps We Took, Length of Each Training Period, Rewards Given for Successes)

_____
_____
_____
_____
_____
_____
_____
_____
_____
_____
_____
_____
_____
_____
_____
_____
_____
_____

_____

_____

_____

_____

_____

_____

What We Accomplished and What Needs More Work

_____

_____

_____

_____

_____

_____

_____

_____

_____

_____

_____

_____

_____

_____

Questions or Concerns

_____

_____

_____

_____

Class 2 Training: Week 2, Day 1

Goals for Second Week

_____

_____

_____

_____

_____

Long-Term Goals

_____

_____

_____

_____

_____

What Was Done or Learned During This Class

_____

_____

_____

_____

_____

_____

_____

_____

_____

_____

_____

_____

_____

Assignment for Next Week's Class

_____

_____

_____

_____

_____

_____

_____

What I Need to Focus on With My Dog

_____

_____

_____

_____

_____

_____

_____

_____

_____

_____

_____

_____

_____

_____

_____

_____

_____

_____

Week 2, Day 2

Goals for the Day

_____

_____

_____

_____

_____

_____

Training (What We Did Today, Steps We Took, Length of Each Training Period, Rewards Given for Successes)

_____

_____

_____

_____

_____

_____

_____

_____

_____

_____

_____

_____

_____

_____

_____

_____

_____

_____

_____

_____

_____

_____

What We Accomplished and What Needs More Work

_____

_____

_____

_____

_____

_____

_____

_____

_____

_____

_____

_____

_____

_____

_____

Questions or Concerns

_____

_____

_____

_____

Week 2, Day 3

Goals for the Day

_____

_____

_____

_____

_____

_____

Training (What We Did Today, Steps We Took, Length of Each Training Period, Rewards Given for Successes)

_____

_____

_____

_____

_____

_____

_____

_____

_____

_____

_____

_____

_____

_____

_____

_____

_____

_____

_____

_____

_____

_____

_____

What We Accomplished and What Needs More Work

_____

_____

_____

_____

_____

_____

_____

_____

_____

_____

_____

_____

_____

_____

_____

Questions or Concerns

_____

_____

_____

_____

Week 2, Day 4

Goals for the Day

_____

_____

_____

_____

_____

_____

Training (What We Did Today, Steps We Took, Length of Each Training Period, Rewards Given for Successes)

_____

_____

_____

_____

_____

_____

_____

_____

_____

_____

_____

_____

_____

_____

_____

_____

_____

_____

_____

_____

_____

_____

What We Accomplished and What Needs More Work

_____

_____

_____

_____

_____

_____

_____

_____

_____

_____

_____

_____

_____

_____

_____

Questions or Concerns

_____

_____

_____

_____

Week 2, Day 5

Goals for the Day

_____

_____

_____

_____

_____

Training (What We Did Today, Steps We Took, Length of Each Training Period, Rewards Given for Successes)

_____

_____

_____

_____

_____

_____

_____

_____

_____

_____

_____

_____

_____

_____

_____

_____

_____

_____

_____

_____

_____

_____

_____

What We Accomplished and What Needs More Work

_____

_____

_____

_____

_____

_____

_____

_____

_____

_____

_____

_____

_____

_____

_____

_____

Questions or Concerns

_____

_____

_____

_____

Week 2, Day 6

Goals for the Day

_____

_____

_____

_____

_____

Training (What We Did Today, Steps We Took, Length of Each Training Period, Rewards Given for Successes)

_____

_____

_____

_____

_____

_____

_____

_____

_____

_____

_____

_____

_____

_____

_____

_____

_____

_____

_____

_____

_____

_____

_____

What We Accomplished and What Needs More Work

_____

_____

_____

_____

_____

_____

_____

_____

_____

_____

_____

_____

_____

_____

Questions or Concerns

_____

_____

_____

_____

Week 2, Day 7

Goals for the Day

_____

_____

_____

_____

_____

_____

Training (What We Did Today, Steps We Took, Length of Each Training Period, Rewards Given for Successes)

_____

_____

_____

_____

_____

_____

_____

_____

_____

_____

_____

_____

_____

_____

_____

_____

_____

_____
_____
_____
_____
_____
_____

What We Accomplished and What Needs More Work

_____
_____
_____
_____
_____
_____
_____
_____
_____
_____
_____
_____
_____
_____
_____
_____

Questions or Concerns

_____
_____
_____
_____

Class 3 Training: Week 3, Day 1

Goals for Third Week

_____

_____

_____

_____

_____

Long-Term Goals

_____

_____

_____

_____

What Was Done or Learned During This Class

_____

_____

_____

_____

_____

_____

_____

_____

_____

_____

_____

_____

Assignment for Next Week's Class

_____
_____
_____
_____
_____
_____
_____

What I Need to Focus on With My Dog

_____
_____
_____
_____
_____
_____
_____
_____
_____
_____
_____
_____
_____
_____
_____
_____
_____
_____
_____

Week 3, Day 2

Goals for the Day

_____

_____

_____

_____

_____

_____

Training (What We Did Today, Steps We Took, Length of Each Training Period, Rewards Given for Successes)

_____

_____

_____

_____

_____

_____

_____

_____

_____

_____

_____

_____

_____

_____

_____

_____

_____

_____

_____

_____

_____

_____

_____

_____

What We Accomplished and What Needs More Work

_____

_____

_____

_____

_____

_____

_____

_____

_____

_____

_____

_____

_____

_____

Questions or Concerns

_____

_____

_____

_____

Week 3, Day 3

Goals for the Day

_____

_____

_____

_____

_____

_____

Training (What We Did Today, Steps We Took, Length of Each Training Period, Rewards Given for Successes)

_____

_____

_____

_____

_____

_____

_____

_____

_____

_____

_____

_____

_____

_____

_____

_____

_____

_____

_____

_____

_____

_____

_____

_____

What We Accomplished and What Needs More Work

_____

_____

_____

_____

_____

_____

_____

_____

_____

_____

_____

_____

_____

_____

_____

Questions or Concerns

_____

_____

_____

_____

Week 3, Day 4

Goals for the Day

_____

_____

_____

_____

_____

_____

Training (What We Did Today, Steps We Took, Length of Each Training Period, Rewards Given for Successes)

_____

_____

_____

_____

_____

_____

_____

_____

_____

_____

_____

_____

_____

_____

_____

_____

_____

_____

_____

_____

_____

_____

_____

_____

What We Accomplished and What Needs More Work

_____

_____

_____

_____

_____

_____

_____

_____

_____

_____

_____

_____

_____

_____

_____

_____

Questions or Concerns

_____

_____

_____

_____

Week 3, Day 5

Goals for the Day

_____

_____

_____

_____

_____

_____

Training (What We Did Today, Steps We Took, Length of Each Training Period, Rewards Given for Successes)

_____

_____

_____

_____

_____

_____

_____

_____

_____

_____

_____

_____

_____

_____

_____

_____

_____

_____

_____
_____
_____
_____
_____
_____

What We Accomplished and What Needs More Work

_____
_____
_____
_____
_____
_____
_____
_____
_____
_____
_____
_____
_____
_____
_____
_____
_____
_____

Questions or Concerns

_____
_____
_____
_____

Week 3, Day 6

Goals for the Day

_____

_____

_____

_____

_____

_____

Training (What We Did Today, Steps We Took, Length of Each Training Period, Rewards Given for Successes)

_____

_____

_____

_____

_____

_____

_____

_____

_____

_____

_____

_____

_____

_____

_____

_____

_____

_____

_____

_____

_____

_____

_____

_____

What We Accomplished and What Needs More Work

_____

_____

_____

_____

_____

_____

_____

_____

_____

_____

_____

_____

_____

Questions or Concerns

_____

_____

_____

_____

Week 3, Day 7

Goals for the Day

_____

_____

_____

_____

_____

Training (What We Did Today, Steps We Took, Length of Each Training Period, Rewards Given for Successes)

_____

_____

_____

_____

_____

_____

_____

_____

_____

_____

_____

_____

_____

_____

_____

_____

_____

_____

_____

_____

_____

_____

_____

_____

What We Accomplished and What Needs More Work

_____

_____

_____

_____

_____

_____

_____

_____

_____

_____

_____

_____

_____

_____

_____

Questions or Concerns

_____

_____

_____

_____

Class 4 Training: Week 4, Day 1

Goals for First Week

_____
_____
_____
_____
_____

Long-Term Goals

_____
_____
_____
_____
_____

What Was Done or Learned During This Class

_____
_____
_____
_____
_____
_____
_____
_____
_____
_____
_____
_____

Assignment for Next Week's Class

_____
_____
_____
_____
_____
_____

What I Need to Focus on With My Dog

_____
_____
_____
_____
_____
_____
_____
_____
_____
_____
_____
_____
_____
_____
_____
_____
_____
_____
_____

Week 4, Day 2

Goals for the Day

_____

_____

_____

_____

_____

_____

Training (What We Did Today, Steps We Took, Length of Each Training Period, Rewards Given for Successes)

_____

_____

_____

_____

_____

_____

_____

_____

_____

_____

_____

_____

_____

_____

_____

_____

_____

_____

_____

_____

_____

_____

_____

_____

_____

What We Accomplished and What Needs More Work

_____

_____

_____

_____

_____

_____

_____

_____

_____

_____

_____

_____

_____

_____

_____

_____

Questions or Concerns

_____

_____

_____

_____

Week 4, Day 3

Goals for the Day

_____

_____

_____

_____

_____

_____

Training (What We Did Today, Steps We Took, Length of Each Training Period, Rewards Given for Successes)

_____

_____

_____

_____

_____

_____

_____

_____

_____

_____

_____

_____

_____

_____

_____

_____

_____

_____

_____

_____

_____

_____

_____

What We Accomplished and What Needs More Work

_____

_____

_____

_____

_____

_____

_____

_____

_____

_____

_____

_____

_____

_____

Questions or Concerns

_____

_____

_____

Week 4, Day 4

Goals for the Day

_____
_____
_____
_____
_____

Training (What We Did Today, Steps We Took, Length of Each Training Period, Rewards Given for Successes)

_____
_____
_____
_____
_____
_____
_____
_____
_____
_____
_____
_____
_____
_____
_____
_____
_____
_____
_____

_____

_____

_____

_____

_____

_____

What We Accomplished and What Needs More Work

_____

_____

_____

_____

_____

_____

_____

_____

_____

_____

_____

_____

_____

_____

_____

Questions or Concerns

_____

_____

_____

_____

Week 4, Day 5

Goals for the Day

_____

_____

_____

_____

_____

Training (What We Did Today, Steps We Took, Length of Each Training Period, Rewards Given for Successes)

_____

_____

_____

_____

_____

_____

_____

_____

_____

_____

_____

_____

_____

_____

_____

_____

_____

_____

_____

_____

_____

_____

_____

What We Accomplished and What Needs More Work

_____

_____

_____

_____

_____

_____

_____

_____

_____

_____

_____

_____

_____

Questions or Concerns

_____

_____

_____

_____

Week 4, Day 6

Goals for the Day

_____

_____

_____

_____

_____

_____

Training (What We Did Today, Steps We Took, Length of Each Training Period, Rewards Given for Successes)

_____

_____

_____

_____

_____

_____

_____

_____

_____

_____

_____

_____

_____

_____

_____

_____

_____

_____

_____

_____

_____

_____

What We Accomplished and What Needs More Work

_____

_____

_____

_____

_____

_____

_____

_____

_____

_____

_____

_____

_____

_____

Questions or Concerns

_____

_____

_____

_____

Week 4, Day 7

Goals for the day

_____

_____

_____

_____

_____

_____

Training (What We Did Today, Steps We Took, Length of Each Training Period, Rewards Given for Successes)

_____

_____

_____

_____

_____

_____

_____

_____

_____

_____

_____

_____

_____

_____

_____

_____

_____

_____

_____

_____

_____

_____

_____

What We Accomplished and What Needs More Work

_____

_____

_____

_____

_____

_____

_____

_____

_____

_____

_____

_____

_____

_____

_____

Questions or Concerns

_____

_____

_____

_____

Class 5 Training: Week 5, Day 1

Goals for First Week

_____
_____
_____
_____
_____

Long-Term Goals

_____
_____
_____
_____
_____

What Was Done or Learned During This Class

_____
_____
_____
_____
_____
_____
_____
_____
_____
_____
_____
_____

Assignment for Next Week's Class

_____

_____

_____

_____

_____

_____

_____

What I Need to Focus on With My Dog

_____

_____

_____

_____

_____

_____

_____

_____

_____

_____

_____

_____

_____

_____

_____

_____

_____

_____

_____

Week 5, Day 2

Goals for the Day

_____

_____

_____

_____

_____

_____

Training (What We Did Today, Steps We Took, Length of Each Training Period, Rewards Given for Successes)

_____

_____

_____

_____

_____

_____

_____

_____

_____

_____

_____

_____

_____

_____

_____

_____

_____

_____

_____

_____

_____

_____

_____

What We Accomplished and What Needs More Work

_____

_____

_____

_____

_____

_____

_____

_____

_____

_____

_____

_____

_____

_____

Questions or Concerns

_____

_____

_____

_____

Week 5, Day 3

Goals for the Day

_____

_____

_____

_____

_____

_____

Training (What We Did Today, Steps We Took, Length of Each Training Period, Rewards Given for Successes)

_____

_____

_____

_____

_____

_____

_____

_____

_____

_____

_____

_____

_____

_____

_____

_____

_____

_____

_____

_____

_____

_____

_____

What We Accomplished and What Needs More Work

_____

_____

_____

_____

_____

_____

_____

_____

_____

_____

_____

_____

_____

_____

_____

Questions or Concerns

_____

_____

_____

_____

Week 5, Day 4

Goals for the Day

_____
_____
_____
_____
_____
_____

Training (What We Did Today, Steps We Took, Length of Each Training Period, Rewards Given for Successes)

_____
_____
_____
_____
_____
_____
_____
_____
_____
_____
_____
_____
_____
_____
_____
_____
_____
_____
_____

_____

_____

_____

_____

_____

_____

What We Accomplished and What Needs More Work

_____

_____

_____

_____

_____

_____

_____

_____

_____

_____

_____

_____

_____

_____

_____

Questions or Concerns

_____

_____

_____

_____

Week 5, Day 5

Goals for the Day

_____

_____

_____

_____

_____

_____

Training (What We Did Today, Steps We Took, Length of Each Training Period, Rewards Given for Successes)

_____

_____

_____

_____

_____

_____

_____

_____

_____

_____

_____

_____

_____

_____

_____

_____

_____

_____

_____

_____

_____

_____

_____

What We Accomplished and What Needs More Work

_____

_____

_____

_____

_____

_____

_____

_____

_____

_____

_____

_____

_____

_____

Questions or Concerns

_____

_____

_____

_____

Week 5, Day 6

Goals for the Day

_____

_____

_____

_____

_____

_____

Training (What We Did Today, Steps We Took, Length of Each Training Period, Rewards Given for Successes)

_____

_____

_____

_____

_____

_____

_____

_____

_____

_____

_____

_____

_____

_____

_____

_____

_____

_____

_____

_____

_____

_____

_____

_____

What We Accomplished and What Needs More Work

_____

_____

_____

_____

_____

_____

_____

_____

_____

_____

_____

_____

_____

_____

Questions or Concerns

_____

_____

_____

_____

Week 5, Day 7

Goals for the Day

_____

_____

_____

_____

_____

_____

Training (What We Did Today, Steps We Took, Length of Each Training Period, Rewards Given for Successes)

_____

_____

_____

_____

_____

_____

_____

_____

_____

_____

_____

_____

_____

_____

_____

_____

_____

_____

_____

_____

_____

_____

What We Accomplished and What Needs More Work

_____

_____

_____

_____

_____

_____

_____

_____

_____

_____

_____

_____

_____

_____

Questions or Concerns

_____

_____

_____

_____

Class 6 Training: Week 6, Day 1

Goals for First Week

_____

_____

_____

_____

_____

Long-Term Goals

_____

_____

_____

_____

What Was Done or Learned During This Class

_____

_____

_____

_____

_____

_____

_____

_____

_____

_____

_____

_____

Assignment for Next Week's Class

_____
_____
_____
_____
_____
_____
_____

What I Need to Focus on With My Dog

_____
_____
_____
_____
_____
_____
_____
_____
_____
_____
_____
_____
_____
_____
_____
_____
_____
_____
_____
_____

Week 6, Day 2

Goals for the Day

_____

_____

_____

_____

_____

_____

Training (What We Did Today, Steps We Took, Length of Each Training Period, Rewards Given for Successes)

_____

_____

_____

_____

_____

_____

_____

_____

_____

_____

_____

_____

_____

_____

_____

_____

_____

_____

_____

_____

_____

_____

_____

_____

What We Accomplished and What Needs More Work

_____

_____

_____

_____

_____

_____

_____

_____

_____

_____

_____

_____

_____

_____

Questions or Concerns

_____

_____

_____

_____

Week 6, Day 3

Goals for the Day

_____
_____
_____
_____
_____
_____

Training (What We Did Today, Steps We Took, Length of Each Training Period, Rewards Given for Successes)

_____
_____
_____
_____
_____
_____
_____
_____
_____
_____
_____
_____
_____
_____
_____
_____
_____

_____

_____

_____

_____

_____

_____

What We Accomplished and What Needs More Work

_____

_____

_____

_____

_____

_____

_____

_____

_____

_____

_____

_____

_____

_____

Questions or Concerns

_____

_____

_____

_____

Week 6, Day 4

Goals for the Day

_____

_____

_____

_____

_____

_____

Training (What We Did Today, Steps We Took, Length of Each Training Period, Rewards Given for Successes)

_____

_____

_____

_____

_____

_____

_____

_____

_____

_____

_____

_____

_____

_____

_____

_____

_____

_____

_____

_____

_____

_____

_____

What We Accomplished and What Needs More Work

_____

_____

_____

_____

_____

_____

_____

_____

_____

_____

_____

_____

_____

_____

Questions or Concerns

_____

_____

_____

_____

Week 6, Day 5

Goals for the Day

_____

_____

_____

_____

_____

_____

Training (What We Did Today, Steps We Took, Length of Each Training Period, Rewards Given for Successes)

_____

_____

_____

_____

_____

_____

_____

_____

_____

_____

_____

_____

_____

_____

_____

_____

_____

_____

_____

_____

_____

_____

_____

_____

What We Accomplished and What Needs More Work

_____

_____

_____

_____

_____

_____

_____

_____

_____

_____

_____

_____

_____

_____

_____

Questions or Concerns

_____

_____

_____

_____

Week 6, Day 6

Goals for the Day

_____

_____

_____

_____

_____

_____

Training (What We Did Today, Steps We Took, Length of Each Training Period, Rewards Given for Successes)

_____

_____

_____

_____

_____

_____

_____

_____

_____

_____

_____

_____

_____

_____

_____

_____

_____

_____

_____

_____

_____

_____

_____

What We Accomplished and What Needs More Work

_____

_____

_____

_____

_____

_____

_____

_____

_____

_____

_____

_____

_____

_____

_____

Questions or Concerns

_____

_____

_____

_____

Week 6, Day 7

Goals for the Day

_____
_____
_____
_____
_____
_____

Training (What We Did Today, Steps We Took, Length of Each Training Period, Rewards Given for Successes)

_____
_____
_____
_____
_____
_____
_____
_____
_____
_____
_____
_____
_____
_____
_____
_____
_____
_____

_____

_____

_____

_____

_____

_____

What We Accomplished and What Needs More Work

_____

_____

_____

_____

_____

_____

_____

_____

_____

_____

_____

_____

_____

_____

Questions or Concerns

_____

_____

_____

_____

Class 7 Training: Week 7, Day 1

Goals for First Week

_____
_____
_____
_____
_____

Long-Term Goals

_____
_____
_____
_____
_____

What Was Done or Learned During This Class

_____
_____
_____
_____
_____
_____
_____
_____
_____
_____
_____
_____

Assignment for Next Week's Class

_____

_____

_____

_____

_____

_____

_____

What I Need to Focus on With My Dog

_____

_____

_____

_____

_____

_____

_____

_____

_____

_____

_____

_____

_____

_____

_____

_____

_____

Week 7, Day 2

Goals for the Day

_____

_____

_____

_____

_____

_____

Training (What We Did Today, Steps We Took, Length of Each Training Period, Rewards Given for Successes)

_____

_____

_____

_____

_____

_____

_____

_____

_____

_____

_____

_____

_____

_____

_____

_____

_____

_____

_____

_____

_____

_____

_____

_____

What We Accomplished and What Needs More Work

_____

_____

_____

_____

_____

_____

_____

_____

_____

_____

_____

_____

_____

_____

_____

Questions or Concerns

_____

_____

_____

_____

Week 7, Day 3

Goals for the Day

_____

_____

_____

_____

_____

_____

Training (What We Did Today, Steps We Took, Length of Each Training Period, Rewards Given for Successes)

_____

_____

_____

_____

_____

_____

_____

_____

_____

_____

_____

_____

_____

_____

_____

_____

_____

_____

_____

_____

_____

_____

_____

What We Accomplished and What Needs More Work

_____

_____

_____

_____

_____

_____

_____

_____

_____

_____

_____

_____

_____

Questions or Concerns

_____

_____

_____

_____

Week 7, Day 4

Goals for the Day

_____

_____

_____

_____

_____

_____

Training (What We Did Today, Steps We Took, Length of Each Training Period, Rewards Given for Successes)

_____

_____

_____

_____

_____

_____

_____

_____

_____

_____

_____

_____

_____

_____

_____

_____

_____

_____
_____
_____
_____
_____
_____

What We Accomplished and What Needs More Work

_____
_____
_____
_____
_____
_____
_____
_____
_____
_____
_____
_____
_____
_____

Questions or Concerns

_____
_____
_____
_____

Week 7, Day 5

Goals for the Day

_____

_____

_____

_____

_____

_____

Training (What We Did Today, Steps We Took, Length of Each Training Period, Rewards Given for Successes)

_____

_____

_____

_____

_____

_____

_____

_____

_____

_____

_____

_____

_____

_____

_____

_____

_____

_____

_____

_____

_____

_____

_____

_____

What We Accomplished and What Needs More Work

_____

_____

_____

_____

_____

_____

_____

_____

_____

_____

_____

_____

_____

_____

_____

Questions or Concerns

_____

_____

_____

_____

Week 7, Day 6

Goals for the Day

_____

_____

_____

_____

_____

_____

Training (What We Did Today, Steps We Took, Length of Each Training Period, Rewards Given for Successes)

_____

_____

_____

_____

_____

_____

_____

_____

_____

_____

_____

_____

_____

_____

_____

_____

_____

_____

_____

_____

_____

_____

_____

_____

What We Accomplished and What Needs More Work

_____

_____

_____

_____

_____

_____

_____

_____

_____

_____

_____

_____

_____

_____

Questions or Concerns

_____

_____

_____

_____

Week 7, Day 7

Goals for the Day

_____

_____

_____

_____

_____

_____

Training (What We Did Today, Steps We Took, Length of Each Training Period, Rewards Given for Successes)

_____

_____

_____

_____

_____

_____

_____

_____

_____

_____

_____

_____

_____

_____

_____

_____

_____

_____

_____

_____

_____

_____

What We Accomplished and What Needs More Work

_____

_____

_____

_____

_____

_____

_____

_____

_____

_____

_____

_____

_____

_____

Questions or Concerns

_____

_____

_____

_____

Class 8 Training: Week 8, Day 1

Goals for First Week

_____

_____

_____

_____

_____

Long-Term Goals

_____

_____

_____

_____

_____

What Was Done or Learned During This Class

_____

_____

_____

_____

_____

_____

_____

_____

_____

_____

_____

_____

Assignment for Next Week's Class

_____

_____

_____

_____

_____

_____

_____

What I Need to Focus on With My Dog

_____

_____

_____

_____

_____

_____

_____

_____

_____

_____

_____

_____

_____

_____

_____

_____

_____

_____

Week 8, Day 2

Goals for the Day

_____
_____
_____
_____
_____
_____

Training (What We Did Today, Steps We Took, Length of Each Training Period, Rewards Given for Successes)

_____
_____
_____
_____
_____
_____
_____
_____
_____
_____
_____
_____
_____
_____
_____
_____
_____
_____

_____

_____

_____

_____

_____

_____

What We Accomplished and What Needs More Work

_____

_____

_____

_____

_____

_____

_____

_____

_____

_____

_____

_____

_____

_____

_____

Questions or Concerns

_____

_____

_____

_____

Week 8, Day 3

Goals for the Day

_____

_____

_____

_____

_____

Training (What We Did Today, Steps We Took, Length of Each Training Period, Rewards Given for Successes)

_____

_____

_____

_____

_____

_____

_____

_____

_____

_____

_____

_____

_____

_____

_____

_____

_____

_____

_____

_____

_____

What We Accomplished and What Needs More Work

_____

_____

_____

_____

_____

_____

_____

_____

_____

_____

_____

_____

_____

_____

_____

Questions or Concerns

_____

_____

_____

_____

Week 8, Day 4

Goals for the Day

_____

_____

_____

_____

_____

Training (What We Did Today, Steps We Took, Length of Each Training Period, Rewards Given for Successes)

_____

_____

_____

_____

_____

_____

_____

_____

_____

_____

_____

_____

_____

_____

_____

_____

_____
_____
_____
_____
_____
_____

What We Accomplished and What Needs More Work

_____
_____
_____
_____
_____
_____
_____
_____
_____
_____
_____
_____
_____
_____

Questions or Concerns

_____
_____
_____
_____

Week 8, Day 5

Goals for the Day

_____

_____

_____

_____

_____

_____

Training (What We Did Today, Steps We Took, Length of Each Training Period, Rewards Given for Successes)

_____

_____

_____

_____

_____

_____

_____

_____

_____

_____

_____

_____

_____

_____

_____

_____

_____

_____

_____

_____

_____

_____

_____

_____

What We Accomplished and What Needs More Work

_____

_____

_____

_____

_____

_____

_____

_____

_____

_____

_____

_____

_____

_____

_____

Questions or Concerns

_____

_____

_____

_____

Week 8, Day 6

Goals for the Day

_____

_____

_____

_____

_____

_____

Training (What We Did Today, Steps We Took, Length of Each Training Period, Rewards Given for Successes)

_____

_____

_____

_____

_____

_____

_____

_____

_____

_____

_____

_____

_____

_____

_____

_____

_____

_____

_____

_____

_____

_____

_____

_____

What We Accomplished and What Needs More Work

_____

_____

_____

_____

_____

_____

_____

_____

_____

_____

_____

_____

_____

Questions or Concerns

_____

_____

_____

_____

Week 8, Day 7

Goals for the Day

_____

_____

_____

_____

_____

_____

Training (What We Did Today, Steps We Took, Length of Each Training Period, Rewards Given for Successes)

_____

_____

_____

_____

_____

_____

_____

_____

_____

_____

_____

_____

_____

_____

_____

_____

_____
_____
_____
_____
_____
_____

What We Accomplished and What Needs More Work

_____
_____
_____
_____
_____
_____
_____
_____
_____
_____
_____
_____
_____
_____
_____
_____

Questions or Concerns

_____
_____
_____
_____

Conclusion

Congratulations to you and your dog in completing your Novice Obedience Training. You can take pride in what you've learned and the progress you have made.

Training does not end at this point. Retaining your dog's skills requires continued practice and reinforcement. While reinforcing the skills already acquired, you will want to continue adding more training and skills to your dog's repertory. And when ready, you can enter actual competitions.

A possible next step following completion of this training and earning your CD or Companion Dog title, would be to take the next level course, Open Competition Obedience. Here you would be doing more complicated exercises as you work toward your CDX title.

Allow your dog whatever time he or she needs to master each skill. Above all, keep doing positive training and have fun with your dog. Keep in mind that, no matter how prepared you feel your dog is, anything can happen when you get into the show ring. It's a strange, new, noisy, and probably somewhat confusing environment—at least at first. If things go wrong, the world will not end. Just put in more work on whatever needs reinforcing, and never take anything out on your dog!

Thank you for using my Novice Obedience Training journal. You may find my other training journals on amazon.com.

Summary of Training

Summary of What My Dog and I Learned

_____
_____
_____
_____
_____
_____
_____
_____
_____
_____
_____

Skills That Need More Practice

_____
_____
_____
_____
_____
_____

Our Next Goals

_____
_____
_____
_____

My Dog's Photo on Graduation Day!

Made in the USA
Las Vegas, NV
18 January 2022